Easter
Jokes

Fun Easter Jokes and Riddles for Kids,
Entertainment and Giggles!

Brad Garland

SPECIAL BONUS!

Want These 2 Books For FREE?

Get **FREE**, unlimited access to these and all of our new kids books by joining our community!

Scan W/ Your Camera To Join!

Table of Contents

Introduction

Here comes Peter Cottontail, hopping down the bunny trail…

As winter holiday fun of Christmas, New Year's Eve, and Valentine's Day, all come to close, here comes Easter!

As Easter approaches, the world begins to thaw. After a long and cold winter, we are greeted with new flowers, colorful eggs, and oh-so-much candy and chocolate.

There are many different reasons to celebrate Easter. For example, Christians celebrate Easter as it is the time of year where their savior was crucified, buried, and rose again. Others celebrate Easter as it is a sign that the dreary winter is over and springtime, with all of its new beauty, is coming soon.

Easter is the one holiday every year that is covered with brightly colored pastels. Everything is covered in blues, pinks, yellows, and purples; from eggs, to flowers, to candy.

To keep in the fashion of this brightly colored holiday, here is a book filled with funny and punny Easter jokes and riddles that your kids, and you, will love!

This book includes seven chapters, each with its own joke and punny theme.

Knee-Knocking Knock Knock Jokes

Knock Knock
Who's there?
Funny Jokes
Funny Jokes who?
There are funny jokes in this chapter!

The Punny Easter Bunny
These jokes are egg-cellent!

Tantalizing Tongue Twisters
We bet you can't say them really fast ten times! But you can try.

Classic and Funny Question & Answer Easter Jokes
Question: What do you call good Easter jokes?
Answer: Funny Bunnies!

Ridiculous Rabbit Riddles
Questions that are short and sweet,
like: "What's an animal with four feet?"
Answer us, we beg of you,making you think is what we do?
What are we?
Riddles!

Funny Bunny Stories and Poems
Poetry and longer jokes guaranteed to make your smile hop off of your face.

Fun Facts About Easter
Did you know there is a lot more to Easter than meets the eye?

With that being said, I hope you enjoy this hare-larious book of Easter puns and jokes!

Let's hop to it, shall we?

3

EASTER JOKES
FUN EASTER JOKES AND RIDDLES FOR KIDS, ENTERTAINMENT AND GIGGLES!

Chapter 1
Knee-Knocking Knock Knock Jokes

Knock! Knock!
Who's there?
Egg
Egg who?
Egg-cited to meet me, are ya?

Knock! Knock!
Who's there?
Alma!
Alma who?
Alma candy is gone already!

Knock! Knock!
Who's there?
Boo!
Boo who?
Cheer up! Don't Cry! It's Easter!

Knock! Knock!
Who's there?
I Sherwood.
I Sherwood who?
I Sherwood like some more chocolate, please!

Knock! Knock!
Who's there?
Some Bunny!
Some Bunny who?
Some Bunny who loves you!

Knock! Knock!
Who's there?
Police!
Police who?
Could you police tell me where you hid the eggs?

Knock! Knock!
Who's there?
Arthur!
Arthur who?
Arthur any more chocolate eggs left?

Knock! Knock!
Who's there?
Egg!
Eggs who?
Egg-cellent question! Where am I?

EASTER JOKES
FUN EASTER JOKES AND RIDDLES FOR KIDS, ENTERTAINMENT AND GIGGLES!

4

Knock, knock!
Who's there?
Dozen.
Dozen who?
Dozen anyone want to find eggs yet?

Knock! Knock!
Who's there?
Anna.
Anna Who?
Anna other Easter Bunny!

Knock, knock!
Who's there?
Easter Egg.
Easter egg who?
You crack me up!

Knock, knock!
Who's there?
Stella.
Stella who?
Stella nother Easter bunny.

Knock, knock!
Who's there?
Harvey.
Harvey who?
Harvey good Easter everyone.

Knock, knock!
Who's there?
Turner.
Turner who?
Turner-ound! It's another Easter Bunny.

Knock, knock!
Who's there?
I'm Heidi
I'm Heidi who?
I'm Heidi the eggs around the house.

Knock! Knock!
Who's there?
Orange.
Orange who?
Orange you glad it's not another Easter Bunny?

Knock, knock!
Who's there?
Jimmy.
Jimmy who?
Jimmy some more candy, please!

Knock! Knock!
Who's there?
Howie.
Howie who?
Howie going to find all of these eggs?

Knock! Knock!
Who's there?
Anne.
Anne who?
Anne Easter Bunny!

Knock! Knock!
Who's there?
Butcher.
Butcher who?
Butcher Eggs in the basket!

Knock! Knock!
Who's there?
Hans.
Hans who?
Hans off my Easter candy!

Knock, knock!
Who's there?
Dewey.
Dewey who?
Dewey have to listen to any more Easter jokes?

Knock! Knock!
Who's there?
Tommy.
Tommy who?
Tommy aches from eating too many Easter jelly beans.

Knock, knock!
Who's there?
Justin.
Justin who?
Justin time to do the Bunny Hop.

Knock, knock!
Who's there?
Wendy.
Wendy who?
Wendy Easter Bunny coming?

Knock, knock!
Who's there?
Are you Donna?
Are you Donna who?
Are you donna want to decorate some eggs?

Knock Knock!
Who's there?
Bea.
Bea who?
Bea kind on Easter.

Knock, knock!
Who's there?
Esther.
Esther who?
Esther Easter Bunny coming?

Knock Knock!
Who's there?
Berlin.
Berlin who?
Berlin the water for hard-boiled Easter eggs.

Knock! Knock!
Who's there?
Donut.
Donut who?
Donut forget to say Happy Easter!

Knock Knock!
Who's there?
Bing.
Bing who?
Bing me some candy, please, Mr. Easter bunny.

Knock Knock!
Who's there?
Freddie.
Freddie who?
Freddie for Easter.

Knock Knock!
Who's there?
Handsome.
Handsome who?
Handsome Easter candy to me, please.

Knock Knock!
Who's there?
Fiona.
Fiona who?
Fiona look out for the Easter Bunny.

Knock, knock!
Who's there?
Chuck.
Chuck who?
Chuck-olate Easter bunnies are my favorite.

Knock Knock!
Who's there?
Harris.
Harris who?
Harris another word for bunny!

Knock Knock!
Who's there?
Zeke.
Zeke who?
Zeke and you shall find Easter eggs!

Knock Knock!
Who's there?
Hayden.
Hayden who?
Hayden eggs on Easter is fun!

Knock Knock!
Who's there?
Holly.
Holly who?
Holly-lujah – it's Easter!

Knock Knock!
Who's there?
Hominy.
Hominy who?
Hominy Easter eggs did you find?

EASTER JOKES
FUN EASTER JOKES AND RIDDLES FOR KIDS, ENTERTAINMENT AND GIGGLES!

Chapter 2
The Punny Easter Bunny

Why shouldn't you tickle an egg?
Because he might crack up!

What kind of stories does the Easter Bunny like?
Ones with a hoppy ending.

How does the Easter Bunny stay healthy?
He egg-ercises!

Why did the Easter Bunny wear a hat?
Because he was having a bad hare day!

What did one Easter egg say to the other?
Have you heard any good yolks lately?

What happened after the Easter Bunny got married?
He lived hop-pily ever after.

What do you call a line of rabbits walking backward?
A receding hare-line.

Why couldn't the rabbit fly home for Easter?
He didn't have the hare fare.

What do you say to the Easter Bunny on his birthday?
Hoppy Birthday.

Why didn't the Easter Egg go into the hot tub?
He didn't want to come out hard boiled.

Who do you call when you have an infestation of eggs?
The egg-sterminator.

What do you call a sleepy Easter egg?
Egg-zosted.

EASTER JOKES
FUN EASTER JOKES AND RIDDLES FOR KIDS, ENTERTAINMENT AND GIGGLES!

8

What do you call a mischievous Easter Egg?
A practical yolker.

How can you make Easter preparations go faster?
Use the eggs-press lane!

Where does the Easter Bunny go when his tail doesn't fit?
To a tail-or.

What does the Easter Bunny say when it burps?
"Eggs-cuse me!"

Where does the Easter Bunny get his eggs?
From an eggplant!

Why can't eggs be comedians?
They'd crack each other up.

What do you call an Easter Bunny with a bad memory?
A hare-brain!

Why didn't the bunny bring eggs?
He just didn't carrot all.

What do you call an Easter Bunny who gets kicked out of school?
Egg-spelled.

Where do bunnies study medicine?
Johns Hop-kins University.

What is the Easter Bunny's favorite dance move?
The Bunny Hop.

What did the Easter Bunny say to the carrot?
It had been nice gnawing on you.

What kind of bunny can't hop?
A chocolate bunny.

How does the Easter Bunny travel?
By Hare-plane.

What's the Easter Bunny's favorite sport?
Basket-ball.

How does the Easter Bunny dry his fur?
With a hare dryer!

What do you call an Easter egg from outer space?
An egg-straterrestrial!

How does the Easter Bunny keep his fur shiny?
With hare spray!

Where does Easter take place every year?
Where eggs mark the spot!

What part did the egg play in the movies?
He was an eggs-tra.

What did the Easter Bunny do after his wedding?
He went on a nice bunny-moon.

What's the best way to send a letter to the Easter Bunny?
Hare-mail!

Why don't you see dinosaurs at Easter?
Because they are eggs-tinct.

Why did the Easter Bunny get a ticket?
He ran a hop-sign.

What did the bunny want to do when he grew up?
Join the Hare Force.

Where do female bunnies hang out?
The hare salon.

EASTER JOKES
FUN EASTER JOKES AND RIDDLES FOR KIDS, ENTERTAINMENT AND GIGGLES!

10

Chapter 3
Tantalizing Tongue Twisters

Try to not get your tongue too twisted! And don't forget, say them ten times and as fast as you can!

- Every Easter, Ella eats eight Easter eggs.

- The funny bunny is chummy with mummy.

- Rabbits ride on round wheels.

- The busy bunny brings baskets.

- Six chicks sit with sticks.

- Jumping jelly beans jiggle and giggle.

- Dancing ducks don't doddle.

- Sweet spring smells.

- Huge hare hopping home.

- Candy coated cotton balls - yuck!

- Charlie chews chewy chocolate.

- Bouncing bunny buys bon-bons.

- April ate Easter almonds.

- Delightful daisies, daffodils and daylilies.

- Eric eats every egg always.

- The fair hare shares and cares.

- Giant giggling golden goose.

- Harry hunts for hidden hideaways.

- The little lamb likes little lilies.
- Pretty peeps paint patterns.
- The red rabbit runs.
- Spring brings pretty things.
- Tulips take time to turn.
- The yellow fellow bellows, "Hello!"
- Peter picks prickly chicks.
- Mandy thinks candy is dandy.
- Crunchy candied carrots.
- March marshmallows make Moms mad.
- Baby chicks chuckle brightly.
- Elegant Easter eggs.
- Colorful chicks chirp cheerfully.
- The funny bunny loves honey.
- Flowers shower you with power.
- The nose knows where the rose goes.
- Exciting expertise in egg excellence.
- Ducklings decorate delicate doilies.
- Esters sister's Easter supper.
- The green grass grows with flowers on the ground.
- Happy Easter to my mister and sister.
- Sunny bunny being funny.
- Ducklings dig for daffodils

EASTER JOKES
FUN EASTER JOKES AND RIDDLES FOR KIDS, ENTERTAINMENT AND GIGGLES!

12

Chapter 4
Classic and Funny Question & Answer Easter Jokes

Question: What kind of beans does the Easter Bunny grow in his garden?
Answer: Jelly beans!

Question: How do you know carrots are good for your eyes?
Answer: Have you ever seen a rabbit with glasses?

Question: What is a rabbit's favorite dance?
Answer: The Bunny Hop.

Question: What kind of diamonds do bunnies wear?
Answer: As many carrots as possible!

Question: Why did the Easter egg hide?
Answer: He was a little chicken.

Question: How does a rabbit make gold soup?
Answer: He begins with 24 carrots.

Question: What is the difference between a crazy bunny and a fake dollar bill?
Answer: One is bad money and the other is a mad bunny!

Question: Why did the chicken cross the road?
Answer: To hide his eggs from the Easter Bunny.

Question: Why did the Easter Bunny cross the road?
Answer: To follow the chicken.

Question: When does Valentine's Day come after Easter?
Answer: In the dictionary.

Question: Where is the Easter Bunny's favorite place to eat?
Answer: IHOP.

Question: Why do we paint Easter eggs?
Answer: Because it's better than wallpapering them!

Question: How many Easter eggs can you put in an empty basket?
Answer: Just one, because then it wouldn't be empty anymore.

Question: How does Easter end?
Answer: With an 'R'.

Question: What do rabbits do when they get caught in the rain?
Answer: They get wet.

Question: Why isn't the Easter Bunny a stand-up comic?
Answer: Because he's not a funny bunny.

Question: Why do bunnies hop?
Answer: Because they can't drive.

Question: Which side of the Easter Bunny has the most fur?
Answer: The outside!

Question: Why don't Easter eggs walk down dark streets at night?
Answer: Because they don't want to get beat.

Question: I was going to tell you a joke about an egg…
Answer: …but it's not all it's cracked up to be.

Question: What happens when the Easter Bunny loses his temper?
Answer: He gets hoppin' mad!

Question: How do you make rabbit stew?
Answer: Make it wait for four hours.

Question: What day does an Easter egg hate the most?
Answer: Fry-days.

Question: Did you hear about the bunny who sat on a bumblebee?
Answer: Don't ask him, it's a sore spot for him.

Question: What happens if you tell a joke to an Easter egg?
Answer: It cracks up.

Question: What did the Easter egg ask for at the hair salon?
Answer: A new dye-job.

Question: How is the liberty bell like an Easter egg?
Answer: They both are cracked!

Question: Why is a bunny the luckiest animal?
Answer: Because it has four rabbit's feet.

Question: What's the best way to make Easter easier?
Answer: Put an "i" where the "t" is.

Question: What kind of bunny can't hop?
Answer: One made of chocolate!

Question: How do you catch a rabbit?
Answer: Make a noise like a carrot.

Question: How does the Easter Bunny paint all the Easter eggs?
Answer: He hires Santa's elves during the off-season.

Question: What do you call a bunny with fleas?
Answer: Bugs Bunny.

Question: What does the Easter Bunny get for making a basket?
Answer: Two points, just like everyone else.

Question: How can you tell which bunnies are the oldest?
Answer: Look out for the grey hares.

Question: Why can't a rabbit's nose be 12 inches long?
Answer: Because then it would be a foot!

Question: What do you call a bunny with money?
Answer: A million-hare.

Question: Why are you so tired in April?
Answer: Because you just finished a March.

Question: What do you call a zen egg?
Answer: An ommmmmmlet.

Question: Why did the jelly bean go to school?
Answer: Because he really wanted to be a Smartie.

Question: What kind of vegetable is angry?
Answer: A steamed carrot!

Question: Would February March?
Answer: No, but April May.

Question: What do you call a rabbit with a cold?
Answer: A runny bunny.

Question: How long do baby chicks like to party?
Answer: Around the cluck!

Question: Why are you stuffing all that Easter candy into your mouth?
Answer: Because it doesn't taste as good if I stuff it in my ears.

Question: Where does Dracula keep his Easter candy?
Answer: In his Easter casket.

Question: A man wanted an Easter pet for his daughter. He looked at a baby chick and a baby duck. They were both cute, but he decided to buy the baby chick. Do you know why?
Answer: The baby chick was a little cheaper.

Question: Why didn't the bunny hop?
Answer: No bunny knows.

Question: If a rooster laid an egg on top of a hill, which side would it roll down?
Answer: Neither, roosters don't lay eggs.

Question: What is the Easter Bunny's favorite game?
Answer: Hopscotch.

Question: What do you get if you cross Winnie the Pooh and the Easter Bunny?
Answer: A honey bunny.

Question: How do you know the Easter Bunny liked his trip?
Answer: Because he said it was egg-cellent.

Question: Where did the Easter Bunny learn how to ski?
Answer: The bunny hill.

Question: What is the Easter Bunny's favorite state capital?
Answer: Albunny, New York.

Question: What do you get when you cross Dumbo with the Easter Bunny?
An elephant who always remembers to eat all of his carrots.

Question: How does the Easter Bunny's day always end?
Answer: With a Y.

Question: Where do Easter Bunnies dance?
Answer: At the basketball.

Question: Why is the Easter Bunny so smart?
Answer: He's an egghead.

Question: Why did the Easter Bunny cross the road?
Answer: To prove he wasn't chicken.

Question: How does an Easter chicken bake a cake?
Answer: From scratch.

Question: What do you need if your chocolate eggs mysteriously disappear?
Answer: An eggs-planation.

Question: Why was the father Easter egg so strict?
Answer: He was hard-boiled.

Question: What would you get if you crossed the Easter Bunny with a famous French general?
Answer: Napoleon Bunnyparte!

Question: What do you call a film about the lives of water birds?
Answer: A duckumentary.

Question: What do ducks have for lunch?
Answer: Soup and quackers.

Question: Why is the letter 'A' like a flower?
Answer: A bee comes after it.

Question: What did the grey rabbit say to the blue rabbit?
Answer: Cheer up!

Question: Christmas does come before Easter in one place 0but where?
Answer: The dictionary!

Question: Why did the farmer feed crayons to his chickens?
Answer: He wanted them to lay colored eggs!

Chapter 5
Ridiculous Rabbit Riddles

In March or April,
these things do abound.
A certain bunny,
leaves these on the ground.
What am I?
> Easter Eggs

I'm the time of the year,
that brings holiday cheer
I bring chocolate, candy, and flowers,
we can search for eggs for hours
What am I?
> Easter

I'm an animal,
and I like to hop,
I have Easter eggs,
that I like to drop.
What am I?
> The Easter Bunny

I sprout and pop every spring,
returning every year is kind of my thing,
I'm so many colors, I stand pretty and tall,
I'll stay with you until summer hits fall.
What am I?
> Tulips

There's white and milk and dark,
these three types you might eat,
as a type of candy,
it really can't be beat.
What am I?
> Chocolates

Together we celebrate, together we eat,
together we sit for a late-night treat.
We are many apart but one altogether,
we will love each other forever and ever.
What are we?
> Family

Come hide me, then find me,
you're lucky if you can spy me.
I'm camouflaged on the ground,
Be careful, I often can't be found.
What am I?
　　Four Leaf Clovers

People walking row by row,
so many more people to go!
They wave and yell, and dance
and sing,
such an event is a beautiful
thing.
What am I?
　　A Parade

I'm yellow and fluffy, and itty
bitty and small,
when standing on the ground,
I'm not very tall.
With little webbed feet I walk
along the ground,
near ponds and streams, I can be
found.
What am I?
　　Little Baby Duck

I'm wicker, and woven,
and my top is open.
Fill me with chocolate and candy,
my bowl-like shape is rather
handy.
What am I?
　　A Basket

You seek, you search, you look,
they hide,
items lurk in and outside.
Look way up high and way down
low,
Until everything's found;
searching you will go.
What are you doing?
　　Easter Egg Hunt

Sometimes these are hollow,
and have chocolate inside,
Other times they're real,
And you paint their outside.
What am I?
　　Easter Eggs

It can look like a T,
it can look like an X.
They can be found on chains,
hung around people's necks.
What am I?
　　A Cross

You can pick me, or let me grow,
my smell can be followed
wherever I go.
To live I need soil, water, and
some sun,
my colors and appearance can
be quite fun.
What am I?
　　Flowers

Out of the four I come second,
after warmer weather is
beckoned.
I bring rain, and sun, and brand-
new flowers,
although some people dislike my
showers.
What am I?
   Spring Time

Up and down, up and down,
move up and down all around.
Make small little jumps up in the
air,
like a rabbit, this jumping can take
you anywhere.
What are you doing?
   Hopping

Blue, yellow, red, and green,
I come in any color you have ever
seen.
I'm small and chewy so take a
bite,
eat a whole handful? I think you
just might!
What are you eating?
   Jelly Beans

Some people visit on Easter
Sunday,
to celebrate this Easter Holiday.
A building of brick, with altars
and pews,
Where people sing loud on cue.
Where are you?
   At Church

The stone rolled away,
the tomb lay bare,
but the angel said,
I am no longer there.
Who am I?
   Jesus

Pretty colors of pretty dyes,
in the cup the egg will lie,
until you're ready to pull it out,
"What a beautiful color!" you
may shout.
What are you doing?
   Coloring Easter Eggs

Chapter 6
Funny Bunny Stories and Poems

The Farmer and his Wife

One spring morning a farmer and his wife woke to find that the fence and gate of where they kept their bunnies had been broken.

Afraid that the bunnies would get loose and run away, the farmer decided to fix the gate as soon as possible. After he collected his tools, he went out to do his daily chores. From inside the house the farmer's wife watched as her husband struggled to gather the bouncing and hopping bunnies into a different cage, to keep them safe while he fixed the gate.

After watching her husband be unsuccessful for about an hour, the farmer's wife came out with a small can in her hand. As she waved the can over the rabbits, spraying them with the contents, they stopped bouncing and hopping around, and stayed still.

"There," she said to her husband, "now you don't have to herd them into another pen. You just have to fix the fence." Without saying anything else, the farmer's wife walked back to her house with her magic can in her hand.

Astonished and confused by the actions of his wife, the farmer went on with fixing the fence. The rabbits simply stood by and watched. The farmer had learned over the years to not question his wife.

That night at dinner the farmer looked out the window to see that the rabbits still hadn't moved, even though the fence was fixed. He decided to ask his wife,

EASTER JOKES
FUN EASTER JOKES AND RIDDLES FOR KIDS, ENTERTAINMENT AND GIGGLES!

21

"What did you spray onto the rabbits? They aren't moving at all! I was able to fix the fence and none of them ran away! And now they still aren't moving. I'm getting worried."

"Don't be worried," said the farmer's wife, "they'll be fine by tomorrow."

"How can you be so sure?" asked the farmer.

The farmer's wife got up from the table and grabbed the can she had used, and handed it to her husband. Slowly her husband read the label on the can. It read:

Extra hold Hairspray!

Keeping your wild and crazy hairs in place for 24 hours!

The Rabbit Stew

A couple sat down in a new restaurant to eat. Before looking at their menus they asked the waiter what the specials were that day.

"Rabbit Stew!" the waiter said, "The chef's specialty! He marinates the rabbit for 48 hours and simmers the stew for six hours."

The man and the woman looked at each other pleased.

"We'll both have the special!" they said. They were excited for their meal.

When the plates arrived at their table, the woman tasted her stew and sent it straight back.

Never having his food sent back before, the chef was a little annoyed, but he served the woman another bowl and sent it out.

Again, the woman took a sip and sent her stew back. The couple could hear the chef yelling from the kitchen, but still the chef served the woman a new bowl of rabbit stew.

No longer annoyed, but fully angry, the chef came out and yelled at the woman.

"What is the matter with my stew?!" he asked the woman.

"Nothing," said the woman, "There was a hair in my bowl."

Easter Time

Easter brings eggs colored pink and blue,

eggs to be shared with me and you.

Chocolate and candy sure are sweet,

so many treats that are good to eat.

Easter eggs are pretty and funny,

has anyone seen the Easter Bunny?

Great Egg-spectations

The Easter Bunny sat on the chair across from his doctor.

"I don't know Doc," said Easter Bunny, "I just don't feel it this year. I don't have the same sort of energy I had the last few years."

"Well, what are you worried about?" asked the doctor.

"What if the kids don't find all the eggs? What if I don't get them hidden on time? So many people are on diets now - what if the chocolate doesn't get eaten?" the Easter Bunny rambled on.

The doctor waited for a moment, then scribbled something down on his prescription pad.

"What's wrong with me, Doc?" asked the Easter Bunny.

"It sounds like you're experiencing some Eggs-iety."

The Bunny and Turtle

Once upon a time a bunny and a turtle decided to race. The bunny wanted to prove, once and for all, that bunnies were faster than turtles. When the race began the bunny took off hopping away. The turtle called over his friend, Bird.

The turtle asked the bird, "Hey, Bird can you pick me up and fly me to the finish line?"

"Of course," said the bird. The bird picked up the turtle by his shell and flew him all the way to the finish line. After being put back on the ground, the turtle turned around to see the bunny hopping his way past the finish line.

"You cheated!" the bunny shouted.

Needless to say, he was a little hot crossed bunny.

Easter Bunny Hugs and Kisses

That cute little bunny has hopped all day,

delivering baskets for the holiday.

His paws are so tired and his nose, how it itches,

he left you something special to fulfill all your wishes,

lots of cute little Easter bunny hugs and kisses.

Driving Lessons

One Easter morning a father was teaching his sixteen-year-old son how to drive.

All was going well until the son began to turn corners.

"Make sure you watch when going around the corners," the father reminded his son, "and don't go too fast."

Of course, the son didn't listen as he zoomed around a corner. All of a sudden, out of the corner of their eye, they saw a purple bunny hopping out of the bushes. The son swerved to the left, then swerved to the right to avoid the bunny.

"Oh my!" shouted the son, "I almost killed the Easter Bunny!"

His father looked back and said, "Don't worry son, you missed it by a hare."

Rabbit Resources

Two days before Easter, the Easter Bunny sat in the Rabbit Resources Department of his egg decorating company.

"Okay, Mister Easter Bunny," the Rabbit Resources representative said, "Do you know why we had to meet today?"

"No ma'am," said the Easter Bunny.

"We have to discuss your firing of Mr. Fred Duck. He is claiming it wasn't fair."

"I had to! It's only a few days before Easter! I had no choice! I had to fire him!" exclaimed the Easter Bunny.

"And why do you think you had no choice?" asked the Rabbit Resources representative.

"His behavior was unacceptable! He was setting us back in our goals and egg numbers. We can only keep the employees that help us reach our egg decorating quotas," the Easter Bunny explained.

"Can you explain to me exactly what he did wrong?"

Easter Bunny raised his hands over his head in frustration.

"He kept quacking all of the eggs!"

Five Little Easter Eggs

Five little Easter eggs, lovely colors they wore;
(hold up five fingers)
Mother ate the blue one, then there were four.
(bend down one finger)
Four little Easter eggs, two and two, you see;
Daddy ate the red one, then there were three.
(bend down next finger)
Three little Easter eggs, before I knew,
Sister ate the yellow one, then there were two.
(bend down next finger)

Two little Easter eggs; oh, what fun,

Brother ate the purple one, then there was one.

(bend down next finger)

One little Easter egg; see me run!

I ate the very last one, and then there were none.

(bend down last finger)

The Chocolate Easter Bunny

Two chocolate Easter Bunnies sat beside each other talking and catching up.

"How are you feeling?" one bunny asked the other.

"I don't know," the other bunny said, "I'm feeling a little empty and hollow."

The Old Man's Hat

There once was an old man who always wore a bunny on his head. He had spent a large amount of money to train the bunny to stay there all day. Everywhere the man went, the bunny was on his head. The townspeople thought it was very weird for the man to wear a bunny on his head, but they never said anything.

One day a little boy gathered the courage to go up to the old man.

"Excuse me sir," the boy said.

"Yes, my child?" the old man replied.

"I was wondering if I could ask you a question."

The little boy was nervous but he needed to know the answer.

"Go ahead, son!"

"Well, I see you walking around town, and I just have to ask, why do you wear that bunny on your head?"

The old man paused for a moment, smiled, and said,

"Because I'm bald, now I have some hare."

Hop and Stop

The first little rabbit went hop, hop, hop,

I said to the first rabbit, "Stop, stop, stop!"

The second little rabbit went run, run, run,

I said to the second rabbit, "Fun, fun, fun!"

The third little rabbit went thump, thump, thump,

I said to the third rabbit, "Jump, jump, jump!"

The fourth little rabbit went sniff, sniff, snuff,

I said to the fourth rabbit, "That is enough!"

The fifth little rabbit went creep, creep, creep,

I said to the fifth rabbit, "It's time to sleep!"

Which Came First?

Billy Bob woke up on Easter morning, excited to see what the Easter Bunny had left for him.

Billy Bob ran downstairs to say good morning to his parents and started running around the house looking for eggs.

When Billy Bob found all of his eggs, candy, and chocolate he laid it out on the kitchen table to look at it all. The Easter Bunny had left him colored play eggs, chocolate bunnies, and chocolate eggs. All of a sudden Billy Bob stopped and stared down at his candy, with a puzzled look on his face.

"What's the matter son?" asked Billy Bob's father.

"I'm just thinking, Dad," said Billy Bob.

"What are you thinking about?" asked Billy Bob's father.

Billy Bob held up two pieces of candy to his dad and said,

"I'm trying to decide which came first-the chocolate chicken or the chocolate egg!"

EASTER JOKES

27   FUN EASTER JOKES AND RIDDLES FOR KIDS, ENTERTAINMENT AND GIGGLES!

Chapter 7
Fun Facts About Easter

Did You Know ...

- Easter is on a different day every year. It falls on the first Sunday after the full moon, after March 11th (Marie, 2017).

- The holidays of Easter and Halloween are the two holidays with the highest sales for candy every year (McDonough, 2021).

- Back in medieval times, a priest would give one of the choir boys a hard-boiled egg, and the boys would pass it amongst themselves until the clock struck midnight. Then whoever was holding it got to eat it (McDonough, 2021).

- In the Christian tradition, Easter is celebrating the resurrection of Jesus Christ.

- The White House, in The United States, holds an annual Easter Egg hunt every year, since 1878.

- Easter is celebrated by Christians throughout the world. It is the most important of the Christian holidays. It is also celebrated by many other people as a fun spring holiday.

Food for Thought

- Over 16 billion jelly beans, 90 million chocolate bunnies, and 700 marshmallow peeps are made every year to prepare for Easter.
  If you were to eat every single jelly bean, chocolate bunny and marshmallow peep in one year you would have to eat:
  43,835,616 Jelly beans, 246,575 chocolate bunnies, and 1,917, 808 marshmallows.
  Talk about a tummy ache! (Marie, 2017).

Do You Know the Easter Bunny?

- Did you know that the Easter Bunny is from Germany? According to the tradition, in the 1700s a bunny would carry around a small basket filled with sweet baked goods and chocolates to hand out to people on Easter. Eventually, the tradition came over to North America, and all over the world (Marie, 2017).

- Did you know that Easter Bunny's name is different in different parts of the world? The two most popular are Peter Cottontail and Peter Rabbit.

- Did you know some children leave out carrots for the Easter bunny in case he gets hungry? (KidsGen, n.d)

- Did you know that the first story about the Easter Bunny hiding eggs was written in 1680?
  Egg-cellent!

- Eggs are shared at Easter, because they represent new life! During the early Spring, when Easter usually falls, everything begins to sprout again after the winter. Eggs are also used to represent the new life and resurrection of when Jesus rose from the dead in the Christian religion (Marie, 2017).

- Did you know that the largest Easter egg ever made was over 25 feet high! (KidsGen, n.d)

- The largest egg hunt was in 2007, and included 501,00 eggs (Kiertnan, 2019).

Easter by the Numbers

- Did you know that over 50% of people eat the ears off of their chocolate bunnies first (McDonough, 2021).

- Around Easter time, each family spends close to $200 on candy and chocolate alone.

- Eighty percent of parents give their kids Easter candy (Kieran, 2019).

- The heaviest chocolate egg weighed over 15000 lbs!

- The most expensive chocolate bunny is around 50,000 dollars, and is 548,000 calories.

- One hundred and eighty million eggs are bought around Easter time.

- Ten million egg-dying kits are bought around the holiday.

- Fifty-seven percent of Easter celebrators will participate in an Easter Egg hunt.

- Fifty-five percent of Easter celebrators will participate in painting eggs.
  Easter Around the World (Moore, 2019)

- An Easter meal is served in Russia, where each person gets a stick of butter carved as a lamb.

- Instead of chocolate bunnies, in Australia they have chocolate bilbies; a rare marsupial.

- In Finland, children dress up as witches with a hat and broom to hunt for their Easter eggs.

- Around the world, eggs are colored with many different colors, but in Greece, many people only color their eggs with red dye.

- In Bermuda, it is traditional for people to fly kites on the Easter holiday.

- In Norway, it is traditional for families to play Murder Mystery parlor games with their invited guests and visitors over the Easter holiday.

- In Luxembourg, individuals often celebrate Easter by sharing and distributing pretzels to their loved ones.

- In France, around a thousand people get together to create a 4000-egg omelet, that they cook, eat, and share together.

Conclusion

Were some those real moaners and groaners? Or did you find them super interesting? Either way, hope those Easter jokes gave you a good chuckle! These Easter jokes are family friendly, and are guaranteed to make anyone laugh, no matter how old they are.

Although Easter is celebrated in many different ways all over the world, everyone can appreciate a good Easter joke, riddle, or pun: some of these are fun!

Easter is a holiday where family is key. What better way to bring the family together than over a good joke.

Feel free to tell them and share them throughout your Easter weekend. Have a HOPPY Easter!

References

11 Facts About Easter. DoSomething.org. https://www.dosomething.org/us/facts/11-facts-about-easter.

Grisafi, P. (2020, December 2). 100+ Easter Jokes and Puns for All the Funny Bunnies in Your Life. Scary Mommy. https://www.scarymommy.com/best-easter-jokes/

Guetebier, A. (2021, January 12). 26 Hoptacular Easter Jokes for Kids. Red Tricycle. https://redtri.com/easter-jokes-for-kids/slide/6.

Injosoft AB. Easter Knock Knock Jokes. https://www.knockknockjokes.nu/holiday-jokes/easter-jokes/?page=2.

Jeon, H. (2021, January 4). These 30 Egg-Cellent Jokes Will Keep You Hopping Through Easter. Good Housekeeping. https://www.goodhousekeeping.com/holidays/easter-ideas/g31153658/easter-jokes/?slide=9.

KidsGen. Easter Facts for Kids. KidsGen. https://www.kidsgen.com/events/easter/easter_facts.htm.

Kiernan, J. S. (2019, April 16). 2019 Easter Facts & Stats – Church, Candy & Cash. WalletHub. https://wallethub.com/blog/easter-facts/19776.

Marie. (2017, March 9). 10 Fun and Interesting Facts About Easter for Kids - Holidappy - Celebrations. Holidappy. https://holidappy.com/holidays/Easter-Facts-Kids.

McCarthy, N. (2018, March 29). Easter Season by the Numbers [Infographic]. Forbes. https://www.forbes.com/sites/niallmccarthy/2018/03/29/easter-season-by-the-numbers-infographic/?sh=b734f8372e11.

McDonough, L. S. (2021, February 11). Break the Ice at Easter Dinner with These 20 Festive Easter Trivia Facts. Good Housekeeping. https://www.goodhousekeeping.com/holidays/easter-ideas/g5064/easter-facts/

Peter Moore. (2019). The world's 11 craziest Easter traditions. Wanderlust. https://www.wanderlust.co.uk/content/worlds-craziest-easter-traditions/?cmpredirect.

Olivia. (2020, April 13). 25 Easter Riddles and Knock Knock Jokes. This West Coast Mommy. https://thiswestcoastmommy.com/25-easter-riddles-knock-knock-jokes/.

Pepper, S. (2015, March 10). Home. Riddles for Kids. https://riddles-for-kids.org/candy-riddles/.

Southern Living. 40+ Funny Easter Jokes and Puns Everyone Will Love. Southern Living. https://www.southernliving.com/easter/easter-jokes.

Tony. (2019, November 21). 33 Funny Easter Jokes for Kids. Kid Activities. https://kidactivities.net/easter-jokes-kids/.

Printed in Great Britain
by Amazon